FROM NAKEDNESS TO PURPOSE

Rachel Flemming

urbanpress

Urban Press
P.O. Box 8881
Pittsburgh, PA 15221-0881 USA
412.646.2780

www.urbanpress.us

Contents

Introduction

This book is titled *From Nakedness to Purpose* and is in a devotional form describing the bonding and harmonizing relationship of God's Spirit and the spirit of a woman whom He loved—whether she is real or fictitious, I will leave that up to your judgment. She was a woman who was physically and mentally abused, and spiritually lost, a woman who searched for love, struggled greatly, and wore many hats. She was a woman who furthered her education and worked hard and long hours to provide for her family.

This woman, perhaps like many women, nurtured the thought that she was always giving love but not receiving love in return. In addition, she felt she had no identity, no purpose, and no meaning, therefore coming to the conclusion that the life she was living was a blatant lie, concluding it was useless to keep on trying to find love. God's movement of His Holy Spirit, however, resonated within her soul. The divine melodious interchange between the two demonstrates our Father's affectionate love towards his daughter, a love that would transform her.

As a loving Father, He assured her "There is a Time for Everything" and this is "A Time" that she as a "Woman" should share her melody of love, hope, and faith so others may acknowledge and hold close to their heart the value of a "Virtuous Wife" (woman, mother, grandmother). She herself as a woman of virtue had slowed down in her life endeavors.

"What Is It?" that slowed her down long enough to ask that question? Could it have been that she was held in bondage by sin, fear, and stress? According to her testimony, she felt desperate and lost in a world of tremendous disillusionment. This woman confessed that she had condemned herself to sin, causing fear and "Stress" to chew on her inner being. Her only relief was to cry out to God for "Strength," communicating to Him her "Need" for love, meaning, and purpose. She told her heavenly Father she felt entrapped, caught in life's turmoil by a narcissistic society headed to self-destruction, a society that knew not the true value of love. Her love for God, however, motivated her to continue to "Reach" out her hands to serve Him and others; in addition, she continued to pray for a change in her life.

God heard her prayers. He gave her the gifts of love—spiritually-wise and truthful love. In addition, He gave her a heart to write poetry. Through her gift of poetry and His heart of love, she received the power and talent to provide encouraging and uplifting love to many who desired to express their words of affection to those they loved but were unable to do so. One day a special woman came into her life and confirmed that her talent to write poetry was a gift from God. Writing personal poetry moved her to become a visionary, to see things she had formerly been incapable of seeing.

As a visionary she could "Envision" the outcome of her investment in the future of a child or person. She walked "The path" of life, in hopes that many would follow. Her life was meaningful because she suddenly realized who "God Is." God was the center of her joy because of His "Peace in the Garden." His peace allowed her to sleep. One morning upon her "Awakening," she read, the "Bridegroom Praises the Bride," and romance was truly an important part of her life.

She pondered what she had read and thought, He has a "Love That Is Too Deep." While, reflecting on His love, she heard the voice of God calling.

"Lehcar, I am calling My daughters."

Therefore, she began searching for her sisters, proclaiming, "God Is Calling His Daughters" because He desires us to connect our spirits. He said, "Our sins have been forgiven for we have loved much." He said for us "to go in peace." In addition, as His heirs, we are to trust, delight ourselves, commit our ways, and rest in Him. After spiritually connecting with her sisters, she went home to pray.

While praying, a gust of wind blew open her game room door and "A Friend" wistfully dropped in. The friend shared with her His fruits. She said to her friend, "I have often desired to stand on the beach and connect with God," "Let Me" and You go to the beach. Once at the beach, she had a joyful "Conversation with God." He assured her there was a "Heritage" waiting for her and all His believers. She worshipped and praised God by singing "Mary's Song." When she was finished, she heard a voice from heaven singing "A Song of Love." When the song was ended, He "Touched" and kissed her on the brow, validating His love for her, declaring, "You are Christ's, and Christ is [Mine], and now is the time for" "A Woman's Chime."

As she leaves you in "Prayer," her hope is everyone who reads *From Nakedness to Purpose* will acknowledge and hold close to their heart the value of a "Virtuous Wife" (woman, mother, grandmother). Now it is your time to come and follow, as she leads you in her walk with God, through His orchestrated love melody of poems and devotions—written in the movement of the Holy Spirit.

As a bonus, I am including the material in Section II titled "Journey to the River of Life." The content complements what I wrote in Section I and is a good follow up as you grapple with God's love for you. I hope you enjoy and are blessed by this work, which is the culmination of many years of my own journey to wholeness and peace.

Rachel Flemming
Eastover, South Carolina
March 2020

But Ruth said, "Entreat me not to leave you, or to turn back from following after you; for wherever you go, I will go; and wherever you lodge, I will lodge; your people shall be my people, and your God, my God" (Ruth 1:16).

Listen to the resonating sound of the bells chiming,
with every breath of the wind . . .

My daughter there is a time for everything.
Now, come and walk with Me . . .

Section One

From Nakedness to Purpose

A Time for Everything

To everything there is a season,
A time for every purpose under heaven.

A time to be born, and a time to die;
A time to plant, and a time to pluck what is planted;

A time to kill, and a time to heal;
A time to break down, and a time to build up;

A time to weep, and a time to laugh;
A time to mourn, and a time to dance;

A time to cast away stones, and a time to gather stones;
A time to embrace, and a time to refrain from embracing;

A time to gain, and a time to lose;
A time to keep, and a time to throw away;

A time to tear, and a time to sew;
A time to keep silence, and a time to speak;

A time to love, and a time to hate;
A time of war, and a time of peace (Ecclesiastes 3:1-8).

The Lord is good to those whose hope is in Him, to the one who seeks Him; it is good to wait quietly for the salvation of the Lord (Lamentations 3:25-26).

A Time

There will come a time
when a woman needs to chime.

She has given of herself in every way.
Yet others who have not and cannot
find the words to say—
I love you.

As a woman so excellent and strong,
would do little that is wrong.
Why is it hard to say?—
I love you.

You have made each day worth living
by the little things you have given.
Someday someone will say—
I love you.

I love you—
in your time of need.
You have given a lot to me.
I love you, I love you—
Now it is your time to chime.

"When I passed you again and looked upon you;
indeed your time was the time of love;
so I spread my wing over you
and covered your nakedness"
(Ezekiel 16:8).

"You too, now have sorrow;
but I will see you again and your heart will rejoice,
and no one takes your joy away from you"
(John 16:22).

Walk as My Creation

"She shall be called woman" (Genesis 2:23).

The Lord God said, "It is not good for man to be alone. I will make a helper suitable for him" (Genesis 2:18).

Woman

Witty, wondrous, and wise—
Don't be surprised.
Ominous, osculating, outspoken—
She is no token.
Meaningful, mellow, mentor—
She is no mere vendor.
Amorous, awesome, accredited—
There is no way she can be edited.
Nurturing, novice, notable—
She will fight against the improbable.

A Virtuous Wife

Who can find a virtuous wife? For her worth is far above rubies. The heart of her husband safely trusts her; so he will have no lack of gain. She does him good and not evil all the days of her life. She seeks wool and flax, and willingly works with her hands She is like the merchant ships, she brings her food from afar. She also rises while it is yet night, and provides food for her household, and a portion for her maidservants. She considers a field and buys it; from her profits she plants a vineyard. She girds herself with strength and strengthens her arms. She perceives that her merchandise is good, and her lamp does not go out by night.

She stretches out her hands to the distaff, and her hand holds the spindle. She extends her hand to the poor, Yes, she reaches out her hands to the needy. She is not afraid of snow for her household, for all her household is clothed with scarlet. She makes tapestry for herself; her clothing is fine linen and purple. Her husband is known in the gates, when he sits among the elders of the land.

She makes linen garments and sells them and supplies sashes for the merchants. Strength and honor are her clothing; she shall rejoice in time to come. She opens her mouth with wisdom, and on her tongue is the law of kindness. She watches over the ways of her household and does not eat the bread of idleness.

Her children rise up and call her blessed;
her husband also, and he praises her:
"Many daughters have done well,
but you excel them all."
Charm is deceitful and beauty is passing,
but a woman who fears the Lord,
she shall be praised.
Give her of the fruit of her hands,
and let her own works praise her in the gates
(Proverbs 31:10-31).

Then each one's praise will come from God
(1 Corinthians 4:5).

What Is It?

Strings you out and makes you want to
scream and shout!

Treats you like a piece of meat;
sits you out for others to eat.

Rips you to shreds wishing you were dead.

Endless as it is.

Sweeping over you.

Slowing you down.
Down
Down
Down

From Nakedness to Purpose

"Come to Me you who labor and are heavy laden,
and I will give you rest.
Take My yoke upon you and learn from Me,
for I am gentle and lowly in heart,
and you will find rest for your souls.
For my yoke is easy and My burden light"
(Matthew 11:28-30).

and know that

"You did not receive the spirit of bondage again to fear,
but you have received the Spirit of adoption,
whereby we cry 'Abba, Father.'
The Spirit bears witness with our spirit
that we are children of God,
and if children, then heirs—
heirs of God and joint heirs with Christ,
if indeed we suffer with Him,
that we may also be glorified together"
(Romans 8:15-17).

Walk as Taught by Me

"Then hear in heaven,
and forgive the sin of Your servants,
Your people Israel,
that You may teach them the good way
in which they should walk;
and send rain on Your land
which You have given to Your people
as an inheritance"
(1 King 8:36).

Strength

Give me the strength.
Give me the strength
to override my fears,
hold back my tears.

You are my fortress and my refuge.
I know what I must do for You.
You are my strength.

"Through the touch of My hands.
I can change the mind of woman and man."
Through Your words of love and truth,
I will bring them nearer to thee.
They too will be free.

With a smile upon my face,
laughter in my heart, they will be aware,
that God is where it begins.
Through me, You live.
You are my strength.

"O Lord, my strength and my fortress, my refuge in
the day of affliction, the Gentiles shall come to You"
(Jeremiah 16:19).

Remember,
My Daughter . . .

"So do not fear, for I am with you;
do not be dismayed, for I am your God.
I will strengthen you and help you;
I will uphold you with my righteous right hand"
(Isaiah 41:10).

A Need

Father, I need You—
I need meaning and purpose in my life.

Father, I need You—
in these moments of confusion.

Father, I need You—
in my moments of pain.

Father, I need You—
yes, I have a need.

Father, I need You—
right now and forever.

Please hear my prayer.

"May my prayer be set before You as incense:
the lifting up of my hands as the evening sacrifice"
(Psalm 141:2).

Walk in My Ways

"But take careful heed to do the commandment
and the law which Moses the servant of the Lord
commanded you, to love the Lord your God,
to walk in all His ways,
to keep His commandments,
to hold fast to Him,
and to serve Him with all your heart
and with all your soul"
(Joshua 22:5).

Reach

Reach out your arms and embrace someone tight,
radiating His love through your soul to theirs,
providing them with foresight.

Loving them with a passion of good taste,
never causing them disgrace,
dancing around in the circle of life.
never worrying about
how much has been sacrificed.

Only that the person you love
with respect and dignity
recognizes you are there,
in the midst of their troubles
and life's complexity.

Be kindly affectionate with one another
with brotherly love,
in honor of giving preference to one another,
not lagging in diligence,
fervent in spirit, serving the Lord;
rejoicing in hope,
patient in tribulation;
continuing steadfastly in prayer;
distributing to the needs of the saints,
given to hospitality (**Romans 12:10-13**).

Walk in My Vision

Then You spoke in a vision to Your holy one and said:
"I have given help to one who is mighty,
I have exalted one chosen from the people"
(Psalm 89:19).

Envision

Envision a time when you and others
will be free to communicate and express.

Not only to set your inner self to rest,
for the time you have to invest.

Visualize the opportunities a child,
a person has in their future.

Intervene and help others with a gift,
to give them a lift.

Surely we are not alone placed in
this position to help in the competition.

Initiate without provocation and provide
a route for revelation.

Out of respect and honor for our
brothers and sisters of color and race.

Not only will the outcome free us
from eradication,
we have given of ourselves to,
get others out of oppression/desperation.

"For you brethren, have been called to liberty; only
do not use liberty as an opportunity for the flesh, but
through love serve one another" (Galatians 5:13).

Walk in the Old Paths

Thus says the LORD: "Stand in the ways and see, and ask for the old paths, where the good way is, And walk in it; Then you will find rest for your souls" (Jeremiah 6:16).

The Path

As I walk down the pathway of life,
I can hear His voice—
so soft, spoken amidst the clouds.

He speaks to me with words
of eminent dependence.
I know I am endowed.

The trees shield and embrace me
in His arms.
The sun beaming upon my head,
guides me and keeps me warm.

I will not lose my direction,
as long as I have His affection.
And yes, I have heard His voice;
And yes, I finally made the choice.

Soon there will be others like me,
walking this path one day,
coming together with one single goal:

To follow Jesus and what He is giving,
so this life will be truly worth living.

"You will show me the path of life; in Your presence
is fullness and joy; at Your right hand are pleasures
forevermore" (Psalm 16:11).

Walk in the Knowledge of Me

Grace and peace be multiplied to you in the knowledge of God and of Jesus our Lord as His divine power has given us all things that pertain to life and godliness, through the knowledge of Him who called us by His glory and virtue (2 Peter 1:2-3).

God Is

God is love God is beauty God is truth

God has placed us here under His roof
to bear living proof
that He lives.

God is love God is beauty God is truth

Yes, He has touched my soul.
Yes, He has touched your soul.
We have been blessed.

God is love God is beauty God is truth

"God is love" (1 John 4:8).

One thing I have desired of the Lord, that will I seek:
That I may dwell in the house of the Lord all the days
of my life, to behold the beauty of the lord. And to
inquire in His temple (Psalm 27:4).

"Father, sanctify them by Your truth.
Your word is truth" (John 17:17).

Walk in My Garden

Now in the place where He was crucified there was a garden, and in the garden a new tomb in which no one had yet been laid (John 19:41).

Peace in the Garden

There is peace in the Garden
even for the hardened.
Sweet peace in the Garden,
we have been pardoned,
when we step into His grace
in the Garden.

Walk as a Child of The Light

For you were once darkness,
but now you are light in the Lord.
Walk as children of the light
(for the fruit of the Spirit is
all goodness, righteousness, and truth)
(Ephesians 5:8-9).

The Awakening

 T oday is the day I was not meant to escape.

It will be a memory to which I will always relate.
I just want to scream and shout;
Thank You, Lord, for bringing to light
what I am about.

My past remembrance is now
our current and future alliance.

I woke up this morning so indulged
in what I must do.

I began thinking and writing of You.
As I read what You guided me to read,
I felt Your breath upon my face.

There is nothing to stop me now;
then I felt Your kiss on my brow.
Yes, Oh Lord, I give You my vow.

I will live forever in Your grace,
with Your impression on my face.

Therefore, He says, "Awake you who sleep,
arise from the dead, and Christ will give you light"
(Ephesians 5:14).

Walk in Love, Following My Son, Jesus Christ

And walk in love,
as Christ also has loved us
and given Himself for us,
an offering and a sacrifice
to God for a sweet-smelling aroma
(Ephesians 5:2).

The Bridegroom
Praises the Bride

Behold, you are fair, my love! Behold, you are fair! You have dove's eyes behind your veil. Your hair is like a flock of goats going down from Mount Gilead. Your teeth are like a flock of shorn sheep which have come up from the washing, every one of which bears twins, and none is barren among them. Your lips are like a strand of scarlet, and your mouth is lovely. Your temples behind your veil are like a piece of pomegranate.

Your neck is like the tower of David, built for an armory, on which hang a thousand bucklers, all shields of mighty men. Your two breasts are like two fawns twins of a gazelle, which feed among the lilies. Until the day breaks and the shadows flee away, I will go my way to the mountain of myrrh and to the hill of frankincense. You are all fair, my love, and there is no spot in you.

Come with me from Lebanon, my spouse, with me from Lebanon. Look from the top of Amana, from the top of Senir and Hermon, from the lions' dens, from the mountains of the leopards.

You have ravished my heart, my sister, my spouse; you have ravished my heart with one look of your eyes, with one link of your necklace. How fair is your love, my sister, my spouse! How much better than wine is your love, and the scent of your perfumes than all spices!

Your lips, O my spouse, drip as the honeycomb; honey and milk are under your tongue; and the fragrance of your garments is like the fragrance of Lebanon. A garden enclosed is my sister, my spouse, a spring shut up, a fountain sealed.

Your plants are an orchard of pomegranates with pleasant fruits, fragrant henna with spikenard, Spikenard and saffron, calamus and cinnamon, with all trees of frankincense, myrrh and aloes, with all the chief spices—a fountain of gardens, a well of living waters, and streams from Lebanon (Song of Solomon 4:1-15).

"He who has the bride, is the bridegroom; but the friend of the bridegroom, who stands and hears him, rejoices greatly, because of the bridegroom's voice. Therefore, this joy of mine is fulfilled" (John 3:29).

A Love That is Too Deep

He is a man of honor, commitment, and integrity.
A standing pillar of love, justice, and mercy.
Gentle, humble, and kind.
He has a love that is too deep—too deep.

Embracing me, not in the ordinary fashion,
He has ignited my passion.
Exciting me with His words of wisdom and truth.
He stimulates me with living proof.
He has a love that is too deep—too deep.

A love that no one can fathom,
a love sent from Heaven.
He has penetrated my soul and my Spirit rejoices.
He could have made many other choices.
He has a love that is too deep—too deep.

He came into my life and released a peace in me.
With Him I feel free.
Agape is the love He has for God,
humanity, and me.
He has a love that is too deep—too deep.

"For God so loved the world that he gave His only
begotten Son, that whoever believes in Him should not
perish but have everlasting life" (John 3:16).

Walk and Listen to My Call

"Listen! The voice,
the cry of the daughter of my people.
from a far country:
Is not the Lord in Zion?
Is not her King in her"?"
(Jeremiah 8:19).

Indeed the Lord has proclaimed
to the end of the world,
"Say to the Daughter of Zion,"
'Surely your salvation is coming,;
behold, his reward is with Him,
and His work is with Him'"
(Isaiah 62:11).

God is Calling His Daughters

God is calling His daughters;
His voice is soft as the wind.

God is calling His daughters,
whose beauty and grace,
reflect His love.

God is calling His daughters,
whose touch of gentleness and kindness prevails.

God is calling His daughters
where His peace dwells.

Come sisters, our Father is calling.
Listen, His voice is soft as the wind.

Come sisters, it is time to connect our spirits.
God, our Father, is calling.

Walk Humbly

Therefore, humble yourselves under the mighty hand of God, that He may exalt you in due time (1 Peter 5:6).

Then he turned to the woman and said to Simon,
"Do you see this woman? I entered your house;
you gave Me no water for My feet, but she has washed
My feet with her tears and wiped them with the hair
of her head. You gave me no kiss, but this woman has
not ceased to kiss my feet since the time I came in. You
did not anoint My head with oil, but this woman has
anointed My feet with fragrant oil. Therefore I say to
you, her sins which are many, are forgiven,
for she loved much. But to whom little is forgiven,
the same loves little." Then he said to her,
"Your sins are forgiven" (Luke 7:44-48).

Heritage – Psalm 37

Do not fret because of evildoers,
Nor be envious of the workers of iniquity.
For they shall soon be cut down like the grass,
And wither as the green herb.
Trust in the Lord, and do good;
Dwell in the land, and feed on His faithfulness.
Delight yourself also in the Lord,
And He shall give you the desires of your heart.
Commit your way to the Lord,
Trust also in Him,
And He shall bring it to pass.
He shall bring forth your righteousness as the light,
And your justice as the noonday.
Rest in the Lord, and wait patiently for Him;
Do not fret because of him who prospers in his way,
Because of the man who brings wicked schemes to pass.
Cease from anger, and forsake wrath;
Do not fret—it only causes harm.
For evildoers shall be cut off;
But those who wait on the Lord,
They shall inherit the earth.
For yet a little while and the wicked shall be no more;
Indeed, you will look carefully for his place,
But it shall be no more.
But the meek shall inherit the earth,
And shall delight themselves in the abundance of peace.
The wicked plots against the just,
And gnashes at him with his teeth.
The Lord laughs at him,

For He sees that his day is coming.
The wicked have drawn the sword
And have bent their bow,
To cast down the poor and needy,
To slay those who are of upright conduct.
Their sword shall enter their own heart,
And their bows shall be broken.
A little that a righteous man has
Is better than the riches of many wicked.
For the arms of the wicked shall be broken,
But the Lord upholds the righteous.
The Lord knows the days of the upright,
And their inheritance shall be forever.
They shall not be ashamed in the evil time,
And in the days of famine they shall be satisfied.
But the wicked shall perish;
And the enemies of the Lord,
Like the splendor of the meadows, shall vanish.
Into smoke they shall vanish away.
The wicked borrows and does not repay,
But the righteous shows mercy and gives.
For those blessed by Him shall inherit the earth,
But those cursed by Him shall be cut off.
The steps of a good man are ordered by the Lord,
And He delights in his way.
Though he fall, he shall not be utterly cast down;
For the Lord upholds him with His hand.
I have been young, and now am old;
Yet I have not seen the righteous forsaken,
Nor his descendants begging bread.
He is ever merciful, and lends;
And his descendants are blessed.
Depart from evil, and do good;
And dwell forevermore.
For the Lord loves justice,
And does not forsake His saints;
They are preserved forever,

But the descendants of the wicked shall be cut off.
The righteous shall inherit the land,
And dwell in it forever.
The mouth of the righteous speaks wisdom,
And his tongue talks of justice.
The law of his God is in his heart;
None of his steps shall slide.
The wicked watches the righteous,
And seeks to slay him.
The Lord will not leave him in his hand,
Nor condemn him when he is judged.
Wait on the Lord,
And keep His way,
And He shall exalt you to inherit the land;
When the wicked are cut off, you shall see it.
I have seen the wicked in great power,
And spreading himself like a native green tree.
Yet he passed away, and behold, he was no more;
Indeed I sought him, but he could not be found.
Mark the blameless man, and observe the upright;
For the future of that man is peace.
But the transgressors shall be destroyed together;
The future of the wicked shall be cut off.
But the salvation of the righteous is from the Lord;
He is their strength in the time of trouble.
And the Lord shall help them and deliver them;
He shall deliver them from the wicked,
And save them, because they trust in Him.

Jesus said to the woman,
"Your faith has saved you, go in peace"
(Luke 7:50).

Walk not After the Flesh but After the Spirit

There is therefore now no condemnation to those who are in Christ Jesus, who do not walk according to the flesh, but according to the Spirit (**Romans 8:1**).

Where can I go from Your spirit? Or where can I flee from Your presence? If I ascend into heaven, You are there; If I make my bed in hell, behold, You are there. If I take the wings of the morning, and dwell in the uttermost parts of the sea. Even there your hand shall lead me, And Your right hand shall hold me, If I say, "surely the darkness shall fall on me," even the night shall be light about me; Indeed, the darkness shall not hide from You, but the night shines as the day; The darkness and the light are both alike to You. For You formed my inward parts; You covered me in my mother's womb (**Psalm 139:7-13**).

A Friend

I feel someone hovering over me.
Can it be a friend, my friend,
my friend the Holy Spirit?
Come right in.

Sit down and be my friend.
So, You say this is not the end,
my friend.

This does not happen often,
when a friend just blows in.

"May the God of hope fill you with joy and peace in
believing, that you may abound in hope by the power
of the Holy Spirit" (**Romans 15:13**).

"That He would grant you, according to His riches in
glory to be strengthened with might by His Spirit in the
inner man (**Ephesians 3:16**).

Walk in
Abundant Praise
of My Love and Majesty

Psalm 145

I will exalt you, my God the King;
I will praise your name for ever and ever.
Every day I will praise you
and extol your name for ever and ever.
Great is the Lord and most worthy of praise;
his greatness no one can fathom.
One generation commends your works to another;
they tell of your mighty acts.
They speak of the glorious splendor of your majesty—
and I will meditate on your wonderful works.
They tell of the power of your awesome works—
and I will proclaim your great deeds.
They celebrate your abundant goodness
and joyfully sing of your righteousness.
The Lord is gracious and compassionate,
slow to anger and rich in love.
The Lord is good to all;
he has compassion on all he has made.
All your works praise you, Lord;
your faithful people extol you.
They tell of the glory of your kingdom
and speak of your might,

From Nakedness to Purpose

so that all people may know of your mighty acts
and the glorious splendor of your kingdom.
Your kingdom is an everlasting kingdom,
and your dominion endures through all generations.
The Lord is trustworthy in all he promises
and faithful in all he does.
The Lord upholds all who fall
and lifts up all who are bowed down.
The eyes of all look to you,
and you give them their food at the proper time.
You open your hand
and satisfy the desires of every living thing.
The Lord is righteous in all his ways
and faithful in all he does.
The Lord is near to all who call on him,
to all who call on him in truth.
He fulfills the desires of those who fear him;
he hears their cry and saves them.
The Lord watches over all who love him,
but all the wicked he will destroy.
My mouth will speak in praise of the Lord.
Let every creature praise his holy name
for ever and ever.

Let Me

Let me stand on the ocean sand,
and overlook the calm waters at sunrise.

Let me feel what it is like to be free
with Your Spirit in me.

Let me stand and gaze at the waves,
moving in an ever-flowing, pulsating,
throbbing beat.

Let me lift up my hands and touch Yours.
Oh Lord, 'tis Thee I adore.

"Rejoice the soul of Your servant, for to You, Oh Lord, I
lift up my soul" (Psalm 86:4).

Conversation with God

I am having a conversation with God;
to some this might seem odd.

To some it is nothing new.
To me it is peace and serenity.
He is telling me something,
of which I must agree is true.

I trust in Him,
so I talk with Him,
and I walk with Him.

I am having a conversation with God.

But you, beloved, building yourselves up on your most
holy faith, praying in the Holy Spirit, keep yourselves
in the love of God, looking for the mercy of our Lord
Jesus Christ unto eternal life (Jude 20-21).

Mary's Song

"My soul magnifies the Lord,
And my spirit has rejoiced in God my Savior.
For He has regarded the lowly state of His maidservant;
For behold, henceforth
all generations will call me blessed.
For He who is mighty has done great things for me,
And holy is His name.
And His mercy is on those who fear Him
From generation to generation.
He has shown strength with His arm;
He has scattered the proud
in the imagination of their hearts.
He has put down the mighty from their thrones,
And exalted the lowly.
He has filled the hungry with good things,
And the rich He has sent away empty.
He has helped His servant Israel,
In remembrance of His mercy,
As He spoke to our fathers,
To Abraham and to his seed forever"
(Luke 1:46-55).

I will sing of the Lord's great love forever; with my mouth I will make faithfulness known through all generations (Psalm 89:1).

Song of Love – Psalm 45

My heart is overflowing with a good theme;
I recite my composition concerning the King;
My tongue is the pen of a ready writer.
You are fairer than the sons of men;
Grace is poured upon Your lips;
Therefore God has blessed You forever.
Gird Your sword upon Your thigh, O Mighty One,
With Your glory and Your majesty.
And in Your majesty ride prosperously because of
truth, humility, and righteousness;
And Your right hand shall teach You awesome things.
Your arrows are sharp in
the heart of the King's enemies;
The peoples fall under You.
Your throne, O God, is forever and ever;
A scepter of righteousness
is the scepter of Your kingdom.
You love righteousness and hate wickedness;
Therefore God, Your God, has anointed You
With the oil of gladness more than Your companions.
All Your garments are scented
with myrrh and aloes and cassia,
Out of the ivory palaces,
by which they have made You glad.
Kings' daughters are among Your honorable women;
At Your right hand stands
the queen in gold from Ophir.
Listen, O daughter,
Consider and incline your ear;

Forget your own people also, and your father's house;
So the King will greatly desire your beauty;
Because He is your Lord, worship Him.
And the daughter of Tyre will come with a gift;
The rich among the people will seek your favor.
The royal daughter is all glorious within the palace;
Her clothing is woven with gold.
She shall be brought to the King
in robes of many colors;
The virgins, her companions who follow her,
shall be brought to You.
With gladness and rejoicing they shall be brought;
They shall enter the King's palace.
Instead of Your fathers shall be Your sons,
Whom You shall make princes in all the earth.
I will make Your name
to be remembered in all generations;
Therefore the people shall praise You forever and ever.

From Nakedness to Purpose

Walk in the Newness of Life

Therefore we were buried with Him through baptism into death, that just as Christ was raised from the dead by the glory of the Father, even so we also should walk in newness of life (Romans 6:3).

Touched

Jesus, Jesus touched my heart.
Jesus, Jesus touched my mind.
Jesus, Jesus touched my soul.
His kiss, I will always remember.
His love, so tender.
Now I can live every day, every moment,
every hour, and every second in His glory.
Glory to glory,
transforming love.

"Be known to unto you all, and all the people of Israel,
that by the Name of Jesus Christ of Nazareth, whom
you crucified, whom God raised from the dead, even by
Him this man stand here before you whole. This is the
stone which was rejected by you builders, which has
become the chief cornerstone. Nor is there salvation
in any other; for there is no other name under heaven
given among men, by which we must be saved"
(Acts 4:10-12).

Jesus, Jesus touched my heart.
Jesus, Jesus touched my mind.
Jesus, Jesus touched my soul.
Glory to glory,
transforming love.

And you are Christ's, and Christ is God's
(1 Corinthians 3:23).

Now Continue to Walk Worthy of Me

... that you may walk worthy of the Lord, fully pleasing Him, being fruitful in every good work and increasing in the knowledge of God (Colossians 1:10).

A Woman's Chime

Yes, it is time for a woman's chime.
For she has taken a lot of physical and
mental abuse.

Yes, it is time for a woman's chime,
so she will never have to say again,
"Life is a lie" or "What's the use?"

She has given love and expressed
her deepest sensitivity,
and she was left without her identity.

Now it is time for a woman's chime,
to invest in herself and seek within.
In this she will gain the greatest wealth.
Her strength, body, and soul now renewed,
refreshed in the spirit and in health.

Yes, it is time for a woman's chime.

"Yes, I swore an oath with you and entered into a
covenant with you, and you became Mine"
(Ezekiel 16:8).

"For this very purpose I have raised you up, that I may
show My power in You, and that my name may be
declared in all the earth" (Romans 9:17).

From Nakedness to Purpose

Finally, My Daughter, Walk in Prayer, Praying in Christ's Name

"And whatever you ask in My name, that I will do, that the Father may be glorified in the son. If you ask anything in My name, I will do" (John 14:13-14).

"By day the Lord directs His love, at night His song is with me—A prayer to the God of my life" (Psalm 42:8).

Prayer

Father, You are an awesome, loving, caring Father who desires the best for His daughters. Father, I pray for strength, wholeness, peace, and love to come to all Your children, but right now, I pray for all the women in the world, both young and old, to come to You in holiness and purity. I pray, Father, that they would be blessed with every spiritual blessing and also filled with the Holy Spirit in order to do Your will.

I pray, Father, that You awaken those who are asleep so they can connect with You and other sisters who believe in Your Son, my Brother, my King, and the lover of our souls, to strengthen and encourage those in need and help them discover how beautifully and wonderfully made they are. And how valuable they are to You.

May they excel in everything that they do. May they become, as Your daughters, virtuous women who will chime like loud resonating bells, proclaiming Your love, Your glory, and honor throughout Your Kingdom here on earth. Father, I ask You to keep them as the apple of Your eye and shield them under Your wing. This is my prayer, in Jesus' name. Amen.

From Nakedness to Purpose

THE

RIVER

OF

LIFE

JOURNEY TO
THE RIVER OF LIFE

Then the angel showed me the river of the water of
life, as clear as crystal, flowing from the throne of God
and of the Lamb down the middle of the great street of
the city. On each side of the river stood the tree of life,
bearing twelve crops of fruit, yielding its fruit every
month. And the leaves of the tree are for the healing
of the nations. No longer will there be any curse. The
throne of God and of the Lamb will be in the city; his
servants will serve him. They will see His face, and
His name will be on their foreheads. There will be no
more night. They will not need the light of a lamp or
the light of the sun, for the Lord God will give them
light and they will reign forever and ever
(Revelation 22:1-5).

Getting to the "River of life" is a difficult, soul-
searching challenge that requires endurance, but God
has predestined it for His saints. To take this journey,
one must follow the path Jesus walked. You must keep
your eyes on the clouds. Study the trees and nature.
Follow the rainbows during and after the rain.

These are all sure signs you are walking on the path,
heading in the right direction for you will be paying
attention and when you pay attention, God can speak
to you. If you should wander off the path Jesus has
chosen, rest assured He will guide you back to the right

path. Just have faith, believe, and pray. God's protecting and guiding love is with you. Ah yes, I almost forgot that there is one very important piece of information you must also have. You must have a heart filled with love to survive and to fulfill this journey—not just love for self but also love for one another. The love of one another is proof that we are children of God (see **1 John 1**).

The only equipment you will need is your Bible, the compass and map for
all directions and paths that can get you to your destination. Lost or full of
questions? Read and study your Bible. Jesus, your Counselor and Guide,
will reveal and explain it to you throughout your journey. The journey is not easy. You will suffer and pick up your cross as you follow Him, but you will be reborn again to live the life God has planned for you. Throughout this journey you will be spiritually conformed into the image of God.

Love is patient and kind; love is not jealous or boastful; it is not arrogant or rude. Love does not insist on its own way; it is not irritable or resentful; it does not rejoice at wrong, but rejoices in the right. Love bears all things, believes all things, hopes all things and endures all things. Love never ends (**1 Corinthians 13:4-7**).

GOD IS LOVE

Jesus, I see you walking
my way,
Your arms
spread wide.

I see you climbing the mountains
and strolling across the sand.
Your stance is so eloquent.

I see with every step and stride
Someone steps to your side.
Our freedom and peace is near.

I see to that when we meet,
I too will be at your side,
Safe and secure in your love.

Welcome into the arms of Jesus, our Savior and Guide.
May God bless those who read and follow His words.
This is my gift from God to you.

"... A pencil in the hand of God ..." Mother Teresa

MEETING JESUS

When we meet Jesus, we are in much need.

"Jesus, please be our Guide.
We are in need of a trusting,
loving, forgiving, kindly,
strong, wise, and truthful leader."

"I, Jesus, the bearer of your burdens,
am your leader and
Counselor. Subject yourself to be like Me.
Prepare to suffer, be persecuted, and die like Me.
Don't only follow Me
but also be like Me
as we journey to "The River of Life."

"Know this about me:

"I am trustworthy, commanding, compassionate
and sympathetic. It is said that I am charming.
I am powerful."

My Father has given me authority over all things"
(John 10:19).

"I am affectionate. I am cheerful.
Children and adults gravitate to me.
I am a pillar of strength, poise and grace."
"Do you desire to share these same characteristics?"

"Do you want to know who you are?"

"Do you desire to see our Father's face?"

"If so, your journey to the 'River of Life'
is going to be a sanctifying and gratifying experience.
A journey that will change your
worldly way of thinking, feeling, and doing.
You will be forgiven of your sins and given grace.
As you further travel on our journey,
you will be molded and conformed into
the spiritual image of My Father, your Creator."

"You are given the choice to follow me.
I cannot force you to come."
"If this is indeed what you want, you will soon hear,
'The Spirit and the Bride say, Come!
And let Him who hears say, Come!
Whoever is thirsty, let him come ++and whoever
wishes, let him take the free gift of the water of life'"
(Revelation 22:17).

"Now follow Me—Jesus.
Our journey to 'The River of Life' begins."

ALONG THE PATH

When we walk with Jesus,
we will have many questions.

"Jesus, you say we are to be made and conformed to the
image of our Father, God. How can that be so?
They say, God is not human but then we are human."
God is perfection,creator of life, night and day.
He is our Lord!"

"Questions my children, answers I have.
"My Father is human through Me His Son.
I live like you. I am tired, sad, hungry, and loving.

"I am both God and man."

"Jesus, we are afraid of the darkness
it makes us uncomfortable,
we cannot see and
we will surely stumble on the rocks."

"Do not fear our path is will lit
as long as you follow me.
For our God as long as I follow,
love, and continue to give my life for you"
(see John 8:12).

"Promise us, Jesus,
You will get us to our destination safely."

"I tell you by the covenant of my Father,
our path taken is part of an ongoing promise

between God and man.
It is known that man (you)
shall go through tests, trials, and purification
until you are refined into the spiritual 'Image of God.'
I promise, God will not leave you."

"Tell us Jesus what to expect
regarding these tests, trials,
and the purification process?
When and how will they take place?"

"My, children I cannot inform you
of my Father's plans.
As James will explain to you,
you should greet your trials with joy,
for they are a test of your faith,
which will develop perseverance
(see James 1:2-3).

"These experiences can
teach you endurance and patience.
They promote the spiritual bond of trust
and your faith in our Father.
This is why you need Me as your guide.
I alone will see that you make it through these things.

"Listen, I can tell you to keep your faith,
trust in God, be strong in your convictions
and repent of your sins.
Never turn back to from where I am taking you.
Most of all, believe in Me."

Remember, as children of God,
your common goal is to strive for holiness
and to unite as one in Christ, in love."

"Now, be silent and let's rest."

CONTINUING THE JOURNEY

When we follow Jesus we want to know
what must we do to be like Him.

"Jesus, what will we eat and drink?"

"I tell you, not to worry about what to eat or drink.
But seek first His kingdom and His righteousness"
(Matthew 6:33).

"Allow your hearts to be filled with the 'fruit of the
Spirit.' These are love, self-control, patience, joy,
goodness, kindness, meekness, faithfulness. and peace
(Galatians 5:22). Partake of this fruit daily, for they will
nourish you and keep you from your sinful nature."

"Soon, you will also be invited and welcome to unite
as one in expressing thanksgiving and praise, through
Holy Communion. This is the act of sharing, one bread
(my body) and a single cup of wine (my blood). You
may do this as often as you like in memory of me."

"I want you to always be assured that your thirst and
hunger will be satisfied as long as you know me and
follow me. 'I am the bread of life. He who comes to me

will never go hungry, and he who believes in me will never be thirsty' (John 6:35)."

"Jesus, are there any rules or instructions we should know as we continue our travels to the 'River of Life'?"

"Yes, God gave Moses Ten Commandments and other laws for you to follow on your journey. Through these commandments and laws, He tells you what you ought to do. These instructions and laws are found in the first five books in your Bible, which are Genesis, Exodus, Leviticus, Numbers, and Deuteronomy."

"If you should obey these as they are given to you out of love for the Father, your obedience in them will prove you are a child of God.

"These laws are just useful precepts, for you do not live by the Law. You live by the letter of the Spirit of God. These are the commandments that you ought to follow to live the life our Father wants you to live."

You shall have no other gods before me.
You shall not make for yourself an idol in the form of anything in heaven above or on the earth beneath or in the waters below. You shall not bow down to them or worship them; for I, the Lord your God, am a jealous God, punishing the children for the sin of the fathers to the third and fourth generation of those who hate me, but showing love to a thousand generations of those who love me and keep my commandments.

You shall not misuse the name of the Lord your God, for the Lord will not hold anyone guiltless who misuses his name.

Observe the Sabbath day by keeping it holy, as lord

your God has commanded you. Six days you shall labor and do all your work, but the seventh day is a Sabbath to the Lord your God. On it you shall not do any work, neither you, nor your son or daughter, nor you manservant or maidservant, nor your ox, your donkey or any of your animals, nor the alien within your gates, so that your manservant and maidservant may rest, as you do.

Honor your father and your mother as the Lord your God has commanded you, so that you may live long and that it may go well with you.

You shall not murder.
You shall not commit adultery.
You shall not steal.
You shall not give false testimony
against your neighbor.
You shall not covet your neighbor's wife
(Deuteronomy 5:1-11).

"Listen! The two commandments to follow are to love the Lord your God with all your heart, soul, mind and strength and your neighbor as yourself."

"I say to you not one of you will be able to state you have not broken one of these commandments or laws. Although you may try and change the wording to fit your needs, their meaning remains the same. I tell you to search your guilty hearts and examine yourself before examining others and then setting judgment on them. I urge you to remain humble. As I told you, those who are without sin should cast the first stone."

"Remember my Father in heaven is watching you. He is the one who will bring judgment upon all."

"Jesus, it is true some of these commandments
and laws we have broken.
Will our Father forgive us of our sins?"
"Do not worry as you will soon learn that My blood
will purify you from sin. Your sins will be forgiven.
Confess them and ask for our Father's forgiveness. God
is a loving and understanding God. He is aware that
the devil will place temptation in front of you."

"James, a servant of God and I Your lord, states,
'When tempted, no one should say, 'God is tempting
me' For God cannot be tempted by evil, nor does He
tempt anyone; but each one is tempted by his own evil
desire, he is dragged away and enticed. Then after the
desire has conceived it gives birth to sin'
(James 1:13-15)."

"But now, I ask you what is sin to you? Is it something
you take lightly or seriously?" Sin is something you
must not take lightly. Listen, as I say unto you. Please
understand, try not to do the sinful things that you have
been forgiven of again and again, and continue to walk
in the light."

"Jesus, who is or what is this devil you speak of?"

"He is linked with sin/evil a fallen angel named
Satan, who tempts us with fleshly, worldly wants,
concerned with ourselves, not others. This evil is found
everywhere. So beware, the lion lurks amongst us to
devour, steal, kill, and destroy."

"As we move on in our journey, I urge you to be
compassionate to one another and others like the
hungry, poor, sick, imprisoned and those who are
treated unjustly this is what love is. If you love them,
you love Me. I also ask you to 'remember the prisoners

as if chained with them, those who are mistreated since you yourselves are in the body also' (Hebrews 13:3)."

"Jesus, what are the things we can do to help the hungry, poor, sick and those who are treated unjustly?"

"Give of yourself and give yourself freely. Be filled with the love of God in mind, heart, and spirit. 'He who gives to the poor will not lack, but He who hides his eyes will have many curses' (Proverbs 28:27)."

"Please pay extra attention to the little children of the world. For I, Jesus love the little children. 'Do not rebuke them. Let the little children come to me, and do not hinder them' (Matthew 19:14)."

"Jesus, what other stops will we make?"

"We will make camp on a mountain where I will present to you my Sermon on the Mount as written in the book of Matthew. Perhaps this will help you understand God's law and the kingdom of God. Further in your travels you will be given an opportunity to repent of your sins and be baptized in the name of the Father, the Son, and the Holy Spirit."

"Jesus why do we have to be baptized? How is it done? What does it mean?"

"Baptism is a religious ceremony in which water is used as a symbol of cleansing from sin. Baptism is a sign that your sins are washed away and I, Jesus, have taken you to be My own. Once baptized you will be filled with the Holy Spirit."

"Jesus, what other things will we learn?"

"There will be many things you will learn as you continue to follow Me. It is hoped that you will be capable of answering that question yourself in testimony to the Father and others; as Lehcar, My servant, is going to do in hopes that you to will see and understand the love, grace, and the power God has.»

"But, before she speaks. I must tell you. I will leave you, but you shall have me in Spirit" I will return again and meet you at 'The River of Life' with My Father.

"Any more questions?"

"Yes, God has loved us so that He has given us you, Prince of Peace, Comforter, our Wonderful Counselor and Healer. Jesus, we know you suffered, carried the cross and died for us. We are sad that you must do these things to save us. In the same breath, we are grateful God sent to us a friend and leader as You. How do we express our gratitude to You and our Father God?"

"I ask you to love the church as I love the church. Do whatever you can to strengthen the spiritual growth and maintain the life of the church. Use the gifts and talents My Father has provided you for the edification of one another and the church. Obey His laws. Remember that the church represents me, Christ. I am the body; you are My parts.

"I also say to you to read your Bible and meditate on His Words, for this is how God speaks to you."

"Pray, for this is the way you communicate with God. Pray for others as well as yourself. Pray for your needs. The Father knows what you need before you ask Him. Do not worry if you do not know how to pray.

I, in Spirit will be your intercessor, meaning I will intercede. I will explain to my Father what it is you are trying to say or ask of Him. I understand what is in your heart."

"Also, when you are praying, remember to pray in My name and believe that our Father will answer your prayers. Do not waste your time on worrying what, how, or when they will be answered. 'If you remain in me and my words remain in you, ask whatever you wish, and it will be given to you' (John 15:7). This is how you should pray:

"Our Father who art in heaven, hallowed be thy name, Thy kingdom come, Thy will be done on earth as it is in heaven. Give us this day our daily bread, forgive our trespassers as we forgive those who trespass against us, lead us not into temptation but deliver us from evil for thine is the kingdom, the power and the glory forever. Amen"

"But now My sheep, listen closely, for now and forever I ask you to worship God!"

"Give God the praise. Glorify His name. For He is all benevolent, magnificent, and awesome. Praise Him in mind and spirit. Love Him with all your heart and soul."

PSALM 150

Praise the Lord.
Praise God in His sanctuary,
Praise him in his mighty heavens.
Praise Him for His acts of power;

Praise Him for His surpassing greatness.
Praise Him with the sounding of the trumpet,
Praise Him with the harp and lyre,
Praise Him with tambourine and dancing,
Praise Him with the strings and flute,

Praise Him with the clash of cymbals,

Praise Him with resounding cymbals.
Let everything that has breath praise the Lord
Praise the Lord.

"In so loving Me, you should set yourself to be a
reflection of His love so that you can save many. For
there are many mansions in my Father's house."

"Be real in your faith, be an example and represent
me and my teachings, because your falsehood could
possibly prevent others from knowing the truth and
experiencing the love of my Father. You can become a
hindrance and a roadblock in their path as they travel
their own journey to the 'River of Life.'"

"Think of Him day and night. Don't only tell Him you love Him. Show Him, which is shown by the way you treat one another. Love one another as you love Him and Me, Jesus. Can you do this?"

"Yes, Jesus!" "As long as we believe in the Father, You the Son, and the Holy Spirit. Jesus, please tell us what the "River of Life" is again?"

"In the words of John, My Father's servant:

Then the angel showed me the river of the water of life, as clear as crystal, flowing from the Throne of God and of the Lamb down the middle of the great street of the city. On each side of the river stood the tree of life, bearing twelve crops of fruit, yielding its fruit every month. And the leaves of the tree are for the healing of the nations. No longer will there be any curse. The Throne of God and of the Lamb will be in the city; His servants will serve him. They will see His face, and His name will be on their foreheads. There will be no more night. They will not need the light of a lamp or the light of the sun, for the Lord God will give them light and they will reign forever and ever (Revelation 22:1-5).

"My children, throughout your journey you will have many questions, cross wide valleys, be caught in many storms, climb treacherous mountains, and walk through hot, sweltering sand. You will be persecuted by many. Be assured God is there and He will send many messengers blessed with truth and faith to your side. They will flourish in His love. They through My Spirit and God's words will get you through it all. Keep the faith and believe!"

"When I leave, I will leave you with a prayer I prayed

to My Father for My believers.
This prayer I prayed before I was arrested and
then crucified for the forgiveness of your sins.
Now I shall leave you with this prayer:

"My prayer is not for them alone. I pray for all those
who will believe in me through their message, that all
of them may be one, Father, just as you are in me and I
in You. May they also be in us so that the world may
believe that you have sent Me. I have given them the
glory that you gave me, that they may be one as we
are one: I in them and you in me. May they be brought
to complete unity to let the world know that you sent
me and have loved them even as you have loved me.
Father, I want those you have given me to be with me
where I am, and to see my glory, the glory you have
given me because you loved me before the creation of
the world.

"Righteous Father, though the world does not know
You, I know you, and they know that you have sent
me. I have made you known to them, and will continue
to make you known in order that the love you have for
me may be in them and that I myself may be in them"
(John 17:20-26).

"Peace and God's blessings, I love you all." "Keep
walking in the light."

Jesus Christ is the same yesterday, today and forever
(Hebrews 13:8).

"I am the Alpha and Omega, the First and the Last,
the beginning and the end" (Revelations 22:13).

RIVER OF PEACE

I am sitting in my chair, but really
I am sitting on the bank of the River of Peace.

Gazing at the picture on the wall, I see Jesus, dressed
in a soft maroon robe,standing across from me on the
bank of the River of Peace.

The mountains, the sun and the clouds blend together
behind the shadow of my Lord. Sitting, I serenely
indulge in His love, right here in my chair, sitting on
the bank of the River of Peace.

I whisper to Him, I love You sweet, sweet Jesus, here
in my chair, sitting on
the bank of the River of Peace.

LEHCAR, GOD'S SERVANT AND AUTHOR OF THIS MESSAGE, NOW SPEAKS

(We will often be called to be a witness of God's love.)

"Lehcar, you may speak."

"Before I begin my testimony Jesus, I would like to thank You for being my guide, my Savior, and the Lover of my soul for without You I would not have made it this far. I am glad to be a witness for You and our Father, God. The journey started out rough and it caused me much despair, hardship, and heartfelt pain. Jesus, it was worth it. I know I have much more to learn so I can continue to be a witness for You as I continue on my journey."

"One more thing—Jesus, I love You."

"Greetings brothers and sisters, I would like to share with you a brief summary of my life up and until now as part of my testimony. I was verbally and physically beaten, manipulated, lied to, discouraged, and led down the wrong path. Some of the perpetrators were people who "loved" me; they unconsciously robbed me of my dignity, self-esteem, self-confidence, and literally stripped me of my strength. Unknowingly, I followed

and placed my trust in these people who did not reflect
God's words and love. I believed in them not ever
thinking what was right or wrong, or understanding
what sin was. In my innocence, I followed what was
before me. Human reasoning and selfishness were my
leaders.

Then one day I stopped at a crossroad and thought, I
am just going in circles. I'm lost. I asked myself, Is this
what life is really about? There has got to be more than
this. Something just doesn't seem right. I felt unreal and
displaced as if I did not belong here on this earth. I felt
I was living a lie, as expressed in this poem I wrote
years ago.

BUILD ME A FORTRESS, LORD

Build me a fortress,
somewhere I can hide,
somewhere I can abide.

Build me a fortress where my
my children can wake without sake.

Build me a fortress before I die,
for life is a lie.

This poem was written on April 15, 1989, eight days
after I was married for the third time. This may have
been the first time I called to God from my heart.

I now know that God had become my fortress as
described in Psalm 91:2, "I will say of the Lord, He is
my refuge and my fortress my God in whom I trust."

As I reviewed the past events and situations in my life, I
know that God had tried many times to help me see the
light and that He was always there protecting me. It was
not until I could finally recognize something was horribly
wrong that He could reach me. I no longer feel like I'm
living a lie. Someday I hope to tell my story on what,
how, and when these events took place. Now it is time
to tell what I have learned so that you may have some
understanding of what is expected of us as Christians.

A word of advice: Understand that God does not conform into us but we into the spiritual image of Him. What have I learned?

I've learned that it is not the words we say
but what we do that proves to others
how the love of God changed our lives.

I've learned I will have my ups and downs and my days will not always go right. I've learned that God answers our prayers when He feels the time is appropriate and sometimes it may not be when we want it. I've learned how easy it is to become judgmental but I am now thankful to know I am not to judge others, but to accept them just as Jesus accepted me, helping them through whatever their needs may be.

I've learned it is important that I teach my children and those whom God places before me about the love He has unselfishly and unconditionally given me and has for them. I've learned to express, and share with them the hope and love Jesus has provided me.

I've learned to observe, listen, and embrace. I've learned to put all concerns, issues, and problems in His hands. I've learned to be calm in the midst of a storm. I've learned that my peace comes from within knowing God is in my presence through the love of Jesus, always giving me strength, guidance, and protection.

I've learned that the devil is always trying to come between the love and goodness of God. I've learned to set aside time to be totally with God. I've learned I am not always open to His will. I've learned I am not perfect and not to expect others to be. I've learned I will sometimes venture from His realm but He will always be there to forgive and bring me back.

I've learned not to do the sinful things I did in the past. I've learned that I should be obedient to His commands. I've learned to separate myself from the worldly way of doing things. I've learned to accept many things as the way God wanted them to be. I've learned God is the sun shining bright and filled with answers. I've learned God is the moon comforting me in the darkness. I've learned He is the star that guides me. I've learned God is very important in the lives of others. I've learned God has been left out in the past. I've learned to be thankful for all things. Most of all I've learned that God is first.

As I further reflect on my journey to "The River of Life," I am aware and grateful I have come a step further spiritually than I and others expected I would come. My self-esteem and self-confidence have become stronger, but not at a level where I would like them to be. Yet in time, I shall meet the desires, of Jesus.

Sometimes, I gaze up at the sky, not in questioning why certain things occurred, but in pure loving gratefulness, realizing how awesome and powerful He is. My tears come in happiness. Father, How Great Thou Art!"

"The River of Life" is where the true worshipers shall meet, united as one in Christ, serving and worshiping our Lord God in spirit and truth (see John 4:23). May the love of God be with us all as we travel in our journey to the "River of Life."

THANK YOU

Thank You, Jesus, for the peace within.
Your sacrifice will live on and on.

Thank You, Jesus, for my deliverance
from sin.

Thank you, for my worldly trials
and tribulations.

Thank You, for Your truth and love.

THE RIVER OF LIFE

Then the angel showed me the river of the water of life, as clear as crystal, flowing from the Throne of God and of the Lamb down the middle of the great street of the city. On each side of the river stood the tree of life, bearing twelve crops of fruit, yielding its fruit every month. And the leaves of the tree are for the healing of the nations. No longer will there be any curse. The Throne of God and of the Lamb will be in the city; his servants will serve him. They will see His face, and His name will be on their foreheads. There will be no more night. They will not need the light of a lamp or the light of the sun, for the Lord God will give them light and they will reign forever and ever (Revelation 22:1-5).

DEDICATIONS

Thank You, Heavenly Father, for being patient and using me as Your messenger. I could not have completed this without Your Holy Spirit. Father, I still have much more work to do to glorify and honor You.

Love,

Your Daughter Rachel

I dedicate " From Nakedness to Purpose" to my daughters: Angelique, Melinda, and Natasha; my son, Aaron; and all the people I had the opportunity to write personal poetry for in my life because of a gift of love from God; to my husband, Odell, for his love and giving me one last name; finally, to my brothers, sisters, cousins, and friends, for their love, prayers, and support.

A special thank you to Carman Warnar-Robbins, who expressed to me that "I had a gift from God" and provided the opportunity for me to publish; and to Dr. Jim Dittmar for telling me "to enjoy my new life."

About the Author
Rachel Flemming

I was born in Detroit Michigan and raised in
Braddock, PA. I graduated with honors, then attended
Community College of Allegheny County in Pittsburgh,
PA. After that, I received a Bachelor of Science Degree
from the University of Pennsylvania, a Master's
Degree in organizational leadership from Geneva
College. I received the Editor's Award for the poem
"A Professional Nurse," published in The National
Library of Poetry; "A Lasting Mirage," in 1997, and
published in "Touched By A Nurse: Special Moments
That Transform Lives" in 1999.

I am a wife, mother, of three daughters and one son,
and a grandmother of fourteen grandchildren, and a
great grandmother. I served as my church's newsletter
editor; I have taught children's Sunday School. I have
ministered to the homeless and to women in a shelter.
I have written personalized poetry for family, friends,
nursing organizations, and churches. I am currently
maintaining a professional nursing career as nurse
manager at C. M. Tucker Nursing Home for Veterans
in Columbia South Carolina.

I love people and I am especially empathetic regarding
the mental, physical, social, and spiritual struggles that
so many women suffer. I know without God and the
power of the Holy Spirit, the victory over these battles

From Nakedness to Purpose

can't be won. My hope is that this inspired melody of poems and devotions will reveal my walk with our heavenly Father on this path of life and also provide healing, encouragement, and spiritual uplifting to all women of the world.
God's peace, joy, and love,

Rachel Flemming

Listen to the resonating sound of the bells
with every breathe of the wind . . .

www.ingramcontent.com/pod-product-compliance
Lightning Source LLC
Chambersburg PA
CBHW062017040426
42447CB00010B/2037